LONGMAN

CORNERSTONE 1

Anna Uhl Chamot

Jim Cummins

Sharroky Hollie

PEARSON
Longman

Longman Cornerstone 1

Pearson Education, 10 Bank Street, White Plains, NY 10606

Staff credits: The people who made up the *Longman Cornerstone* team, representing editorial, production, design, manufacturing, and marketing, are John Ade, Rhea Banker, Liz Barker, Kenna Bourke, Jeffrey Buckner, Brandon Carda, Daniel Comstock, Martina Deignan, Gina DiLillo, Nancy Flaggman, Cate Foley, Patrice Fraccio, Tracy Grenier, Zach Halper, Henry Hild, Sarah Hughes, Karen Kawaguchi, Lucille Kennedy, Ed Lamprich, Jamie Lawrence, Niki Lee, Christopher Leonowicz, Tara Maceyak, Katrinka Moore, Linda Moser, Liza Pleva, Edie Pullman, Monica Rodriguez, Tara Rose, Tania Saiz-Sousa, Chris Siley, Heather St. Clair, Loretta Steeves, and Andrew Vaccaro.

Text design and composition: The Quarasan Group, Inc.
Illustration and photo credits: See page 302.

Library of Congress Cataloging-in-Publication Data
Chamot, Anna Uhl.
　　Longman cornerstone / Anna Uhl Chamot, Jim Cummins, Sharroky Hollie.
　　p. cm. - - (Longman cornerstone; 1)
　　Includes index.
　　1. Language arts (Elementary school)—United States. 2. Language arts
　　(Elementary school)—Activity programs 3. English language—Study and teaching.
　　I. Cummins, Jim II. Hollie, Sharroky III. Title.

ISBN-13: 978-0-13-513597-6
ISBN-10: 0-13-513597-4

Printed in the United States of America

3 4 5 6 7 8 9 10–CRK–12 11 10 09

About the Authors

Anna Uhl Chamot is a professor of secondary education and a faculty advisor for ESL in George Washington University's Department of Teacher Preparation. She has been a researcher and teacher trainer in content-based second-language learning and language-learning strategies. She co-designed and has written extensively about the Cognitive Academic Language Learning Approach (CALLA) and spent seven years implementing the CALLA model in the Arlington Public Schools in Virginia.

Jim Cummins is the Canada Research Chair in the Department of Curriculum, Teaching, and Learning of the Ontario Institute for Studies in Education at the University of Toronto. His research focuses on literacy development in multilingual school contexts, as well as on the potential roles of technology in promoting language and literacy development. His recent publications include: *The International Handbook of English Language Teaching* (co-edited with Chris Davison) and *Literacy, Technology, and Diversity: Teaching for Success in Changing Times* (with Kristin Brown and Dennis Sayers).

Sharroky Hollie is an assistant professor in teacher education at California State University, Dominguez Hills. His expertise is in the field of professional development, African-American education, and second-language methodology. He is an urban literacy visiting professor at Webster University, St. Louis. Sharroky is the Executive Director of the Center for Culturally Responsive Teaching and Learning (CCRTL) and the co-founding director of the nationally-acclaimed Culture and Language Academy of Success (CLAS).

Consultants and Reviewers

Rebecca Anselmo
Sunrise Acres Elementary School
Las Vegas, NV

Ana Applegate
Redlands School District
Redlands, CA

Terri Armstrong
Houston ISD
Houston, TX

Jacqueline Avritt
Riverside County Office of Ed.
Hemet, CA

Mitchell Bobrick
Palm Beach County School
West Palm Beach, FL

Victoria Brioso-Saldala
Broward County Schools
Fort Lauderdale, FL

Brenda Cabarga Schubert
Creekside Elementary School
Salinas, CA

Joshua Ezekiel
Bardin Elementary School
Salinas, CA

Veneshia Gonzalez
Seminole Elementary School
Okeechobee, FL

Carolyn Grigsby
San Francisco Unified School District
San Francisco, CA

Julie Grubbe
Plainfield Consolidated Schools
Chicago, IL

Yasmin Hernandez-Manno
Newark Public Schools
Newark, NJ

Janina Kusielewicz
Clifton Public Schools/Bilingual Ed.
& Basic Skills Instruction Dept.
Clifton, NJ

Mary Helen Lechuga
El Paso ISD
El Paso, TX

Gayle P. Malloy
Randolph School District
Randolph, MA

Randy Payne
Patterson/Taft Elementaries
Mesa, AZ

Marcie L. Schnegelberger
Alisal Union SD
Salinas, CA

Lorraine Smith
Collier County Schools
Naples, FL

Shawna Stoltenborg
Glendale Elementary School
Glen Burnie, MD

Denise Tiffany
West High School
Iowa City, IO

Dear Student,

Welcome to *Longman Cornerstone*!

We wrote *Longman Cornerstone* to help you learn to read, write, and speak English. We wrote a book that will make learning English and learning to read a lot of fun.

Cornerstone includes a mix of all subjects. We have written some make-believe stories and some true stories.

As you use this program, you will build on what you already know, learn new words and new information, and take part in projects. The projects will help you improve your English skills.

Learning a language takes time, but just like learning to swim or ride a two-wheeler, it is fun!

We hope you enjoy *Longman Cornerstone* as much as we enjoyed writing it for you!

Good luck!

Anna Uhl Chamot
Jim Cummins
Sharroky Hollie

Your *Cornerstone* Unit!

Cornerstones are important for building and learning.
This book will help you learn to read, write, and speak English.
Meet your book!

Kick Off Each Unit

❓ Big Question

The Big Question gets you thinking about what is to come.

What Do You Know?

Talk about the unit theme.

Sing

Sing a short song to help you think about the theme.

Begin Each Reading

Vocabulary

Get to know the words *before* you read. Learn the phonics that will help you learn to read, too.

About the Story

Get a sneak peak into what the Reading is all about.

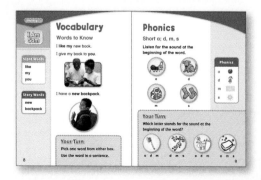

Read the Story

Readings ①, ②, and ③
Read with success!

I am sad.

I am new.

After Each Reading

Think It Over
Answer some questions
about what you just read.

Wrap Up Each Unit

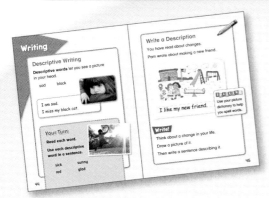

Writing
Learn about writing
and practice writing on
your own.

❓ Wrap Up
Discuss the Big Question
with your class. Choose a
project to work on and share.

Changes

? The **Big** Question

Reading 3

Unit Wrap Up

Unit

2

Contents

Communities

? The Big Question

Traditions

? The **Big** Question

Unit 4

Animals and Plants

Reading 3

Unit Wrap Up

Unit 5

Contents

All Kinds of Americans

xvi

Reading 3

Unit Wrap Up

Unit 6

Contents

Friendships

? The Big Question

Unit 1

Changes

Sometimes change is hard. But sometimes change is fun!

?

The Big Question
How will you change
this year as you meet
new friends?

Let's Talk

Name some things
that change. How
do they change?

3

What Do You Know about Changes?

Children grow.

Flowers bloom.

Weather changes.

We make new friends.

Your Turn

Think about a change in your life. Tell about it.

Sing about Changes

Changing Seasons

In fall, we rake the leaves.

In winter, we play in snow.

All throughout the year,

the seasons come and go.

Flowers grow in spring.

The summer breezes blow.

All throughout the year,

the seasons come and go.

I Am Sam

Vocabulary

Words to Know

I **like my** new book.

I give my book to **you**.

I have a **new backpack**.

Sight Words

like

my

you

Story Words

new

backpack

Your Turn

Pick one word from either box.

Use the word in a sentence.

Phonics

Short a; d, m, s

Listen for the sound at the beginning of the word.

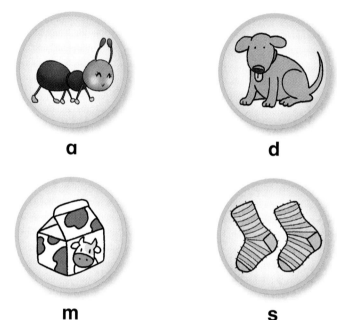

a

d

m

s

Phonics

a

d

m

s

Your Turn

Which letter stands for the sound at the beginning of the word?

a d m   d m s   a d m   a m s

About the Story

Who is in the story?

Sam

mother

Sam

Where does the story happen?

home

school

I Am Sam

by Pamela Walker

illustrated by Kathryn Mitter

I am Sam.

I like my shoes.

I like my backpack.

I am sad.

I am new.

I am Sam.

I am Sam.

 I am happy.

 I love you.

Think It Over

1. What things does Sam have for school?

2. Why is Sam sad?

3. Who does Sam meet at school?

4. How does Sam feel at the end of the story?

I Met Ted

Vocabulary

Words to Know

I **see** a dog.

The dog **is little**.

I see a **butterfly**.

Can you see the **frog**?

Your Turn

Pick one word from either box.

Use the word in a sentence.

Phonics

Short e; f, l, t

Listen for the sound at the beginning of the word.

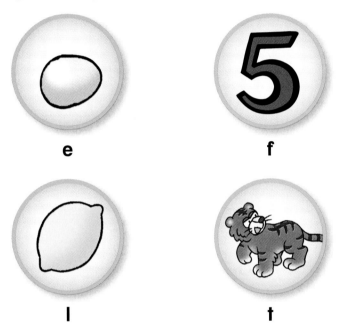

e

f

l

t

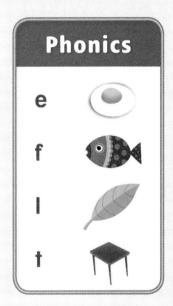

Phonics

e

f

l

t

Your Turn

Which letter stands for the sound at the beginning of the word?

f l t

e f l

e l t

e f t

21

About the Story

Who is in the story?

caterpillar

frog

Where does the story happen?

tree

pond

I Met Ted

by Christian Foley
illustrated by Don Tate

23

I am a caterpillar.

I am little.

I met Ted.

Ted is a tadpole.

See Ted.

Ted is a fat tadpole.

Ted is a fat, fat tadpole.

Ted is big.

Ted sat and sat.

I am at home.

Ted is a frog.

I am a butterfly.

Think It Over

1. How big is the caterpillar at first?

2. How big is the tadpole at first?

3. How does the tadpole change?

4. How does the caterpillar change?

Frogs

1 A frog begins as an egg. ▶

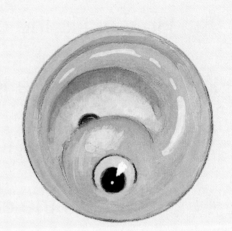

2 It is now a tadpole.

3 Back legs grow. ▶

4 Front legs grow. ▶

▲ **5** It is now a frog.

Activity to Do!

Draw pictures to show change.

- Draw a tadpole.
- Draw a frog.

33

Vocabulary

Words to Know

Do you **have** a snack for **me**?

Sight Words

have

me

too

My hat is **too** big.

Story Words

three

fun

Three pals have **fun**.

Your Turn

Pick one word from either box.

Use the word in a sentence.

Phonics

Short i; n, p

Listen for the sound at the beginning of the word.

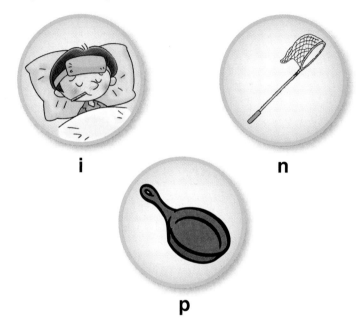

i

n

p

Phonics

i

n

p

Your Turn

Which letter stands for the sound at the beginning of the word?

i p n

i p n

i p n

i p n

About the Story

Who is in the story?

Tip

Nan

Don

pals

Where does the story happen?

city

country

Tip

by Katrinka Moore
illustrated by Mary Roja

I am Tip.

I am sad.

Nan is sad, too.

Nan is a pal.

I can see Nan.

I can sit in Don's van.

I have three new pals.

Ann, Ed, and Mel pet me.

I am not too sad.

I can have fun.

Think It Over

1. Why is Tip sad?

2. What does Tip like to do?

3. What was Tip's old home like?

4. What is Tip's new home like?

Descriptive Writing

Descriptive words let you see a picture in your head.

sad   black

I am sad.

I miss my black cat.

Your Turn

Read each word.

Use each descriptive word in a sentence.

sick   sunny

red   glad

Write a Description

You have read about changes.

Pam wrote about making a new friend.

I like my new friend.

Write!

Think about a change in your life.

Draw a picture of it.

Then write a sentence describing it.

The Big Question

How will you change this year as you meet new friends?

Written

Write about a New Friend

Write a story to tell about a new friend.

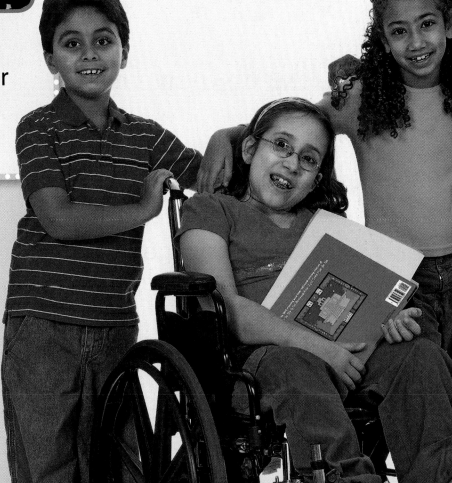

Oral	**Visual/Active**
Introduce a New Friend	**Draw a New Friend**
Introduce a new friend to your class.	Draw pictures to show what your new friend looks like.

Unit 2

Communities

Some communities are big. Some communities are small. We all live in a community.

Visit *LongmanCornerstone.com*

? The **Big** Question

Who are the people who help in your community?

Let's Talk

Tell about three people in your community.

What Do You Know about Communities?

A city is a community.

A bus driver works in a community.

A small
town is a
community.

A teacher works
in a community.

People live and work
in a community.

Your Turn

Think about a place
in your community.
Tell about it.

51

Sing about Communities

People in the Community

The people on the street say,

"Hello, hello, hello."

"Hello, hello, hello."

"Hello, hello, hello."

The people on the street say,

"Hello, hello, hello,"

all over town.

The driver on the bus says,

"Hello, hello, hello."

"Hello, hello, hello."

"Hello, hello, hello."

The driver on the bus says,

"Hello, hello, hello,"

all over town.

Vocabulary

Words to Know

Rosa asks for help.

He can help.

She asks **about** his important job.

People can mail a **letter**.

Sight Words

he

she

about

Story Words

people

letter

Your Turn

Pick a word from either box.

Use the word in a sentence.

Phonics

Short o; c, h

Look at each picture.
Read the word.

hot

doll

on

cat

Phonics

o

c

h

Your Turn

Point to the word that names the picture. Read the word.

dog   dig

hit   fit

pot   pat

hot   cot

About the Story

Who is in this story?

people

Where does the story happen?

community

People Can Help

by Lawrence Po

illustrated by Apryl Stott and Sue Miller

Dot can help Ned send a letter.

Sal can help Mom and Tam.

She can take Mom and Tam on the bus.

Ed can sit at a desk.

He can help get a book
about a cat.

Dan is sad about his
dog, Top.

Nan can help Top.

Tom can help Tim, Pam,
and Ted cross.

A lot of people can help.

Think It Over

1. What does Ned give Dot?

2. Who helps Mom and Tam?

3. Why is Dan sad?

4. How does Tom help the kids?

Bud and His Dad

Vocabulary

Words to Know

Look at **the** man in back.

He passes to **another** man.

Sight Words

look

the

another

This glass of milk is a **delicious snack**.

Story Words

delicious

snack

Your Turn

Pick a word from either box.

Use the word in a sentence.

Phonics

Short u; b, j

Look at each picture.
Read the word.

jam

bus

up

hug

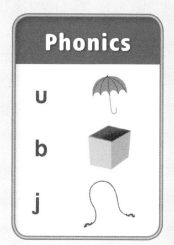

Phonics

u

b

j

Your Turn

Which letter stands for the missing sound?

_ u g

c _ p

_ e d

b _ g

67

About the Story

Who is in the story?

Bud

Dad

Pat

Where does the story happen?

shops

Bud and His Dad

by Denise Lewis

illustrated by Barbara Spurll

Bud and his dad can

hop to the shop.

Bud can have milk and
jam. Bud likes milk and jam
a lot. Mmmm.

Bud and his dad hop to another shop.

Bud and his dad see Pat.

Bud can have another snack.

Mmmm. Mmmm.

Look! A blue snack is on Bud.

Mmmm, it is delicious!

Think It Over

1. Where do Bud and his dad hop?

2. Who do Bud and his dad see at the second shop?

3. What color is Bud's snack?

4. What is on Bud?

Jane Has a Job

Vocabulary

Words to Know

I can **use** **this** pen.

School can **be** fun.

Sight Words

use

this

be

The **doctor** got **mail** today.

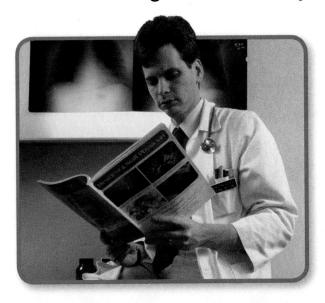

Story Words

doctor

mail

Your Turn

Pick a word from either box.

Use the word in a sentence.

Phonics

Long a; r, w

**Look at each picture.
Read the word.**

plate

flame

wet

run

Phonics

a

r

w

Your Turn

Point to the word that names the picture. Read the word.

wade   made

take   rake

gate   get

77

About the Story

What is the story about?

The story is about Jane.

Jane brings mail to people.

Jane Has a Job

by Cecelia Rice

illustrated by Sue Miller

Jane has a job.

The mail will not be late.

Jane will put this
letter in a red slot.

Jane can hand mail
to Doctor Ron. Doctor
Ron helps pets get well.

Doctor Ron can use
this mail. It will help sick
cats and dogs get well.

Jane has a letter for Rob.

His pal Wes Spade sent it.

Jane can help a lot of people.

Think It Over

1. What does Jane bring to people?

2. What kind of job does Jane have?

3. How did Jane help Doctor Ron?

4. What did Jane have for Rob?

Mailing a Letter

1. Nate can mail a letter. ▶

◀ **2.** Jill can load it in the truck.

3. The letter gets sorted. ▶

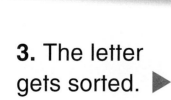

4. Bill will deliver the letter. ▶

▲ **5.** Nat will get the letter from Nate.

Activity to Do!

You can become a mail carrier.

- Write a letter.
- Tell something about your community.
- Deliver your letter to a friend.

87

Writing

Narrative Writing

When you talk about what happens, you tell what you did. Sometimes you can write about what you did.

I went to the shop.

I got a snack.

Your Turn

Read each sentence in the box above.

Which words tell what the person did?

Write a Narrative

You have read about communities.

Bud wrote about his life in a city.

I live in a city.
Sometimes I go to the park.
I went there yesterday.

Write!

Think about one thing you do in your community.

What do you do? When do you do it?

Write about it.

The Big Question

Who are the people who help in your community?

Written

Write about a person in your community

What does the person do? What job does the person have? Write about it.

Oral

Interview a person in your community

Talk to a person in your community who has an interesting job. What makes the job interesting?

Visual/Active

When I Grow Up...

What job in your community would you like to have? Act out how you will do that job.

Unit 3

Traditions

People celebrate traditions. Thanksgiving is a tradition.

Let's Talk

Tell about a tradition in your family.

What Do You Know about Traditions?

People follow traditions.

A Thanksgiving parade
is a tradition.

On Valentine's Day, people give cards to each other.

On the Fourth of July, families have picnics.

Your Turn

Think about your favorite tradition.

Tell about it.

Sing about Traditions

Family Traditions Song

Family, family, get together.

Time to celebrate, all together.

Some have Christmas.

Some have Kwanzaa.

Some have Hanukkah.

Some have Ramadan.

Family, family, get together.

Time to celebrate, all together.

We will eat.

What will you bring?

Gather round

And let us sing.

Family, family, get together.

Time to celebrate, all together.

Vocabulary

Words to Know

We have a red, **white**, and **blue** flag in **our** school.

We live in North **America**.

The **moon** is full.

We learn about the moon at **school**.

Your Turn

Pick one word from either box.

Use the word in a sentence.

Phonics

Long o; g, z

**Look at each picture.
Read the word.**

gate

zip

stove

hole

Phonics

o

g

z

Your Turn

Which letter stands for the sound at the beginning of the word?

g n z

g c z

o g z

o t g

About the Story

What is the story about?

The story is about the American flag.

A Flag

by Bonnie Lee

A flag is red and white and blue
in America! America is our home.

I can see red and white
and blue. It is our flag.

I can see flags.
Flags can stand in my school.
Flags can stand at my home.

I can see flags at games.
A man is glad to stand
with a flag at a game.

A man lands on the moon.

The flag is on a pole.
The man pokes a hole to
get the flag to stand up.

I am at home and safe with
America's flag. I can gaze at it.
It is a beautiful flag!

Think It Over

1. What colors make up the flag in America?

2. Where can flags stand?

3. Why do people wave our flag?

4. Why did the man poke a hole in the moon?

Celebration Time!

Vocabulary

Words to Know

Lots **of** people play at birthday parties.

I like **to** play, too.

I like **green** balloons best.

Sight Words

of

to

green

Story Words

carnival

celebration

costume

A **carnival** is a **celebration**.

People can wear a **costume**.

Your Turn

Pick one word from either box.

Use the word in a sentence.

Phonics

Long i; v, x

**Look at each picture.
Read the word.**

van

ox

five

ride

 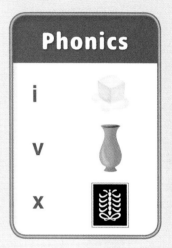
Your Turn

Which letter stands for the sound in the middle of the word?

b __ ke

w __ ve

b __ x

k __ te

111

About the Story

What is the story about?

United States

China

Brazil

Ghana

The story is about celebrations around the world.

Celebration Time!

by Carol Johnson

I can have lots and lots of fun!
It is celebration time!

It's the New Year. It can be
named for an ox, rat, pig, or ram.
Around the world, it is
celebration time!

I can have a fun time at
a carnival.
I can put on a big blue wig
and a mask to hide.

I can smile and dress up.
I can dress up in a red
and green costume.
It is fun to dress up in a hat.

On July 4, I can dress up
in red, white, and blue.
I can wave a flag.

Mom, Dad, and I gaze at the sky.
Pop! Pop! Pop! Pop! Pop! Pop!

In Ghana, tribes plant crops.
It is celebration time.
Lots of drums go tap, tap, tap!

Think It Over

1. What can the New Year be named for?

2. On July 4, what colors does the boy dress up in?

3. Where can people play lots of drums?

4. What sound do the drums make?

Celebrations

China

In China, people dress in dragon costumes to celebrate the New Year. ▶

Brazil

▲ In Brazil, people celebrate Carnival with feasts and parades for days and days.

United States

In the United States, people celebrate Independence Day with fireworks. ▶

Ghana

▲ In Ghana, people celebrate a big harvest of crops at the Homowo festival.

Activity to Do!

Flag Day is a day to celebrate our flag.

- Use paint, crayons, or markers to make a U.S. flag.
- Write a story about our flag.

Thanksgiving Time!

Vocabulary

Words to Know

They go on a ride **first**.

Then they will play **with** friends.

The **Thanksgiving parade** is fun.

They go on a **sleigh**.

Sight Words

first

then

with

Story Words

Thanksgiving

parade

sleigh

Your Turn

Pick one word from either box.

Use the word in a sentence.

Phonics

Long u; k, ck

Look at each picture.
Read the word.

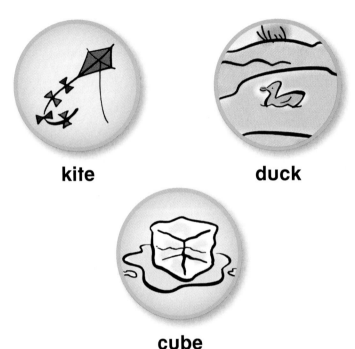

kite

duck

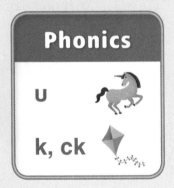

Phonics

u

k, ck

cube

Your Turn

Point to the word that names the picture. Read the word.

use   us   up

kit   kick   kite

sock   sob   spot

About the Story

What is the story about?

The story is about Thanksgiving.

Thanksgiving is a celebration.

Thanksgiving Time!

by Mary O'Donnell

At Thanksgiving time we
used cups and plates.
First we sat and then we ate
and ate and ate.

People came to a new land
to make a home and lend
a hand.

June helps a lot with Jules
and Gram.

And Zack hands Pam
a plate full of yams.

A big parade will pass us by.
I gaze at a star up in the sky.

Then I see big pipes and a drum.
I sing a tune and I hum and hum.

I am glad Ken and
June came.

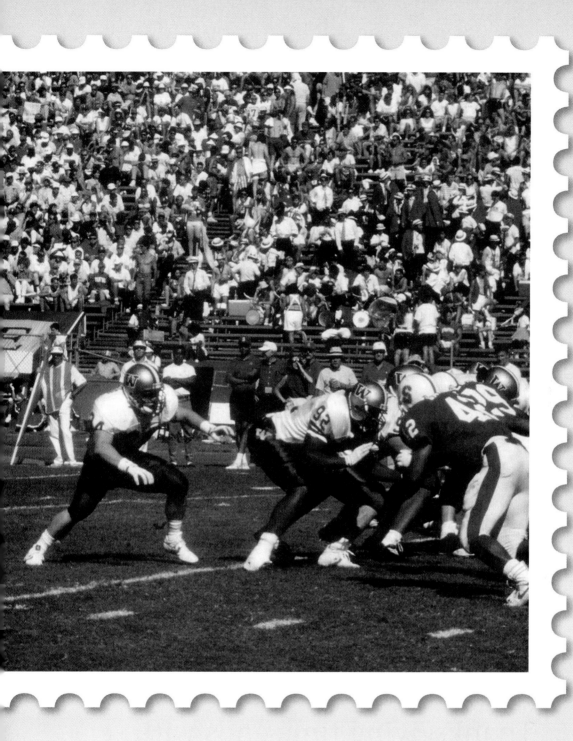

It is fun to see a big
Thanksgiving game.

Thanksgiving time ends with
a fun sleigh ride.
I hum a tune while my family
and pals sit by my side.

Think It Over

1. Who helps Gram?

2. What does Zack pass to Pam?

3. What did Ken and June see?

4. Who went on the sleigh?

Writing

Expository Writing

Expository writing tells about something. You can tell how to do something. You can describe something. You can explain what something is.

People decorate trees
to celebrate Christmas.
Families get together. People give gifts.

Your Turn

Read each sentence. Which sentence tells what Christmas is?

1. Christmas is a celebration.

2. I like Christmas.

3. I went to see my grandmother.

4. People get gifts on Christmas.

Writing Nonfiction

You have read about traditions.

What is your favorite tradition? Tell about it.

    What do people do?

    When do they celebrate?

    Where do they celebrate?

My favorite tradition is
the Fourth of July.
People hang flags.
They wear red, white,
and blue.
Families have picnics.

SPELLING

Names of special celebrations and traditions are capitalized.

Write!

Think about a school celebration. Write about it.

1. When is the celebration?

2. What do you do at the celebration?

The Big Question

What is your favorite way to celebrate?

Written

Write about a family celebration

What do you do? Who is there? Write about it.

Oral

Describe a family celebration

Without saying what the celebration is, describe it. Can your class guess what your family celebration is?

Visual/Active

Draw a picture of a family celebration

Draw a picture that shows your family celebrating.

Unit 4

Animals and Plants

Some plants help animals. Some animals help plants. Living things can help each other.

Visit *LongmanCornerstone.com*

Let's Talk

Tell about plants in your community. Then tell about animals in your community. Do these plants and animals help each other? How?

What Do You Know about Animals and Plants?

I can eat some plants.

We can use trees to make this home.

Plants and animals can help each other.

People can help plants and animals, too.

Animals can be our friends!

Your Turn

Do you have a pet? If you could have any pet, which would you choose? Tell about it.

145

Sing about Animals and Plants

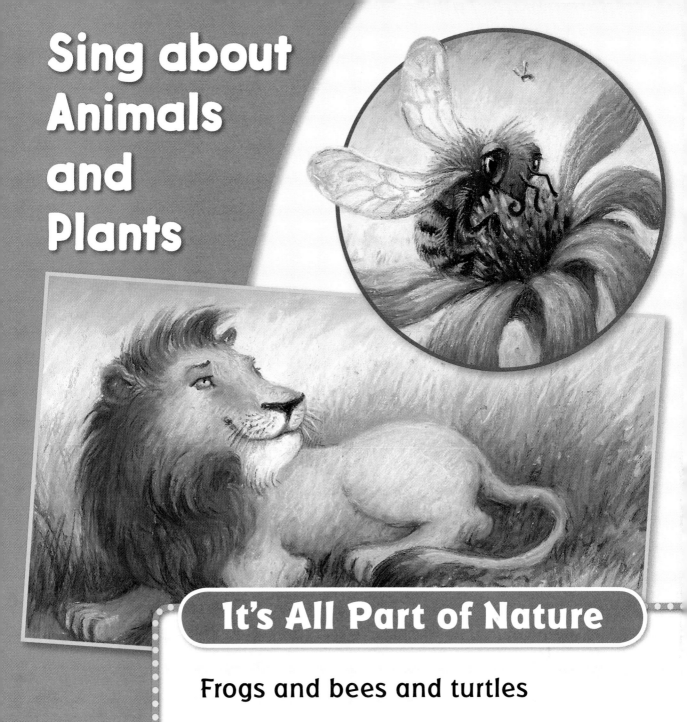

It's All Part of Nature

Frogs and bees and turtles
and fleas,

Lions, bats, and weasels.

Cats and crows, everyone knows,

Are all part of nature!

Trees and grasses across
the land,
Growing ever stronger.
A lovely rose, 1 bet you know,
Is all part of nature!

Vocabulary

Words to Know

Why can I see the bird? It is **because** I look at it with my binoculars.

Sight Words

why
because
so
out

The eagle flies **so** gracefully **out** in the clear blue sky.

Story Words

waddle
duckling
feathers

All the ducks **waddle** along together.

A baby duck is called a **duckling**.

Duck **feathers** are very soft.

Your Turn

Pick one word from either box.

Use the word in a sentence.

148

Phonics

Long e; ch, sh

Look at each picture.
Read the word.

chick

ship

read

Your Turn

Which letter, or letters, stand for the sound at the beginning of the word?

ch   th   sh

ch   sh   dr

a   e   i   o

149

About the Story

Who is in the story?

duckling

duck

Where does the story happen?

pond

Little Duck

by Sarah Beacker

Peep! Peep! Peep! I see a duck.
Why is it so small? It is so small
because it just hatched.

An egg shell cracks. I see feet!
I see a beak! A duckling can get
out of its shell.

A duckling came out of an egg.
It is a cute duckling. But it can
not stand up yet.

Ducks can walk. Ducks waddle
and sway to walk. A duck says,
"Peep! Peep! Peep!"

Ducks check for bugs. Why?
Ducks check for bugs because
ducks like to eat bugs.

Three ducks swim in a big pond.
Ducks can swim. Ducks kick big,
flat feet to swim.

A duck has feathers so it
will not get cold.
Little ducks get big fast!

Think It Over

1. Why is the duckling so small?

2. What does the duckling say?

3. How do ducks swim?

4. Why do ducks check for bugs?

Plants

Vocabulary

Words to Know

Before a plant can **grow**, it needs sunlight.

After sunlight, a plant needs water, too.

The boy adds **water** to his plant. Then a **blossom** will bloom.

I like picking pumpkins in a **pumpkin** patch.

Your Turn

Pick one word from either box.

Use the word in a sentence.

Phonics

Long a; th, y

Look at each picture.
Read the word.

yak

bath

gray

train

Phonics

a

th

y

Your Turn

Point to the word that names the picture. Read the word.

snail   snake

play   pail

yam   yak

About the Story

What is in the story?

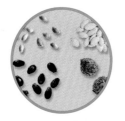
seeds

peach

leaves

carrot

watermelon

pumpkin

flower

What is the story about?

The story is about all kinds of plants.

Plants

by Nikki Pagano
illustrated by Linda Holt Ayriss

Seeds make plants. A seed needs a
lot of rain and a lot of sun before
it can grow big and strong.

You may plant this black seed in wet dirt. After about six days, vines will pop out. A blossom may bloom and then watermelons may grow.

A watermelon is red and green. If you wait, it will get big and sweet. Yum! Yum! Yum!

This seed is named a pit or a stone.
It may grow to be a peach. It will
need a lot of water and sun to help
it grow.

leaves

A peach grows on a tree. Can you see big, green leaves on this peach tree? Pick a peach off a tree. A peach is a sweet treat that tastes as fine as it can. Yum! Yum! Yum! Yum!

Do you see the thin seeds? You may add water and sun to these seeds. A big orange pumpkin will grow and lay on the soft ground.

stem

Pumpkins have thin lines and thick stems. Pumpkins have seeds inside. You may make pumpkins into pie. Mmmmm. Yum! Yum! Yum! Yum!

Think It Over

1. What happens when a seed gets water and sun?

2. Where do peaches grow?

3. What kind of stems do pumpkins have?

4. What colors are a watermelon?

Plants

leaf

stem

root

Carrot ▶
Can you see the parts of a carrot? Name all of its parts.

blossom

leaf

stem

root

▲ **Daisy**
This plant is a daisy.
The blossom is white
and yellow. Name all
of its parts.

Activity to Do!

What is your favorite plant?

- Draw a picture of it.
- Color it.
- Label all of its parts.

173

Living Things

Vocabulary

Words to Know

Many animals live by a pond.

They all live together. It can be **very** crowded.

Sight Words

many

they

all

very

Story Words

living

food chain

birds

All **living** things form a **food chain**.

Birds are part of the food chain.

Your Turn

Pick one word from either box.

Use the word in a sentence.

Phonics

Long i

**Look at each picture.
Read the word.**

cry

night

child

fly

Your Turn

Name the pictures. Which words have the same sound as the *i* in *ice*?

About the Story

What is in the story?

rain

bug

flower

bee

bird

What is the story about?

The story is about living things.

Living Things

by Morgan Carl

illustrated by Drew-Brook Cormack

Many living things need help. All plants need sun and rain. Rain falls on this plant, so it can get big. Bright sunlight is best for most plants.

All bugs must drink. Can plants help bugs? This leaf helps a bug by catching rain. The bug will sip the rain and get big.

Can bugs help plants? Yes! Bees
pick up many plant bits. Plant
bits stick to bees.

Bees find many plant bits. They spread plant bits. The bits help plants grow very big.

Bugs help plants. Birds help plants, too.
Birds eat bugs as a snack.

Birds fly very high in the sky.
Then they can see bugs to eat.

All living things need to eat. Plants need sun and rain water. Bugs find plants to eat. Then bugs eat plants. Birds find bugs to eat. Then birds eat bugs. This is a food chain.

Think It Over

1. Where do plants get water?

2. How do bees help plants?

3. What do bugs eat?

4. What do birds eat?

Writing

Informational Writing

Sometimes, authors write to explain or tell about things. This kind of writing is called **informational writing**.

Seeds need soil and water to grow. Seeds also need sun and a place to grow.

Your Turn

Look at the picture. Which sentence tells you about the leaf and the bug?

1. This bug eats the leaf for food.

2. This bug does not like the leaf.

186

Write Nonfiction

You have read about animals and plants.
What is your favorite animal?
Write about it.

My favorite animal is a frog.
Frogs are green or yellow or
red. Many frogs live near the
pond. They make me
laugh when they say
"Ribbit."

SPELLING

Say a word out
loud to help you
spell it.

Write!

Think about your favorite plant.
What is it? Where have you seen it?
Write about it.

The Big Question

How can living
things help
each other?

Written

Write about
a plant or an
animal.

What does it look like?
What do you like most
about it? How does it
help other things?

Introduce your favorite plant or animal.

Tell the class about your favorite plant or animal. Why do you like it so much?

Be your favorite plant or animal.

Move like your animal as it runs, or move like your plant on a windy day. Make the sounds your animal makes.

Unit 5

All Kinds of Americans

People come from different places. People from many countries come to live in America.

The Big Question

?

What do you like most about living in America?

Let's Talk

Think about the people in your community. Discuss the different countries they came from.

What Do You Know about All Kinds of Americans?

Many people from Puerto Rico live in America.

Many people celebrate Chinese traditions in America.

People brought these dolls from Russia to America.

You can find Jamaican musicians playing this instrument in America.

People brought sushi from Japan to America.

Your Turn

What traditions or foods did your family bring to America? Tell about it.

Sing about All Kinds of Americans

We Are All Americans

It is good; it is good;

it is good in America.

We laugh, we learn,

and we live in harmony.

America is for you and me.

194

It is good; it is good;

it is good in America.

We share, we play,

and we live with peace and love.

America is the land I love.

One, Two, Three, Play!

Vocabulary

Words to Know

I have **one** head and **two** hands.

This boy **wants** you to know he is **from** Pakistan.

My mom **bought** me this **soccer ball**.

Sight Words

one

two

wants

from

Story Words

bought

soccer

ball

Your Turn

Pick one word from either box.

Use the word in a sentence.

Phonics

Long o

Look at each picture.
Read the word.

float   soap

toe   blow

Your Turn

Which letters stand for the sound in the middle
of the word?

oa ay   ai ow   oa ie   ee oa

197

About the Story

Who is in the story?

Blake   **Cliff**   **Joan**   **Joe**

What is the story about?

football

soccer

One, Two, Three, Play!

by Ben Akin

illustrated by Mark Stephens

Blake just bought a football.
He wants to play with Cliff
and Joan. Blake likes to play
in a football game.

Blake can throw and pass. Joan can run fast. Cliff can kick the football. Blake needs one more kid. Then they can play a game.

Can Joe play with Blake and Cliff
and Joan? Joe is from another
land. Joe has not seen a ball like
this. Joe says, "This is not the
same as in my land."

Joe shows Blake, Cliff, and Joan his ball. Blake, Cliff, and Joan tell Joe that it is a soccer ball. Joe says it is named a football in his land. Joe says he likes to play football in his land.

Blake tells Joe that this is
named a soccer ball in his land.
Blake tells Joe that soccer is fun
but football is fun, too. Blake
will teach Joe to play football.

Blake can pass to Joe. One, two, three, the football goes high. Can Joe get the football from Blake? Blake will teach Joe to catch and pass.

Joan shows Joe how to block
and run to the goal line. One,
two, three, Joe runs to the goal
line fast. Joe likes this game.
It is fun.

Cliff wants to play soccer. Cliff wants to kick and run and score. Can Cliff play soccer? Joe can show Cliff how to play. Joe can coach Cliff.

Joe can use his feet to play soccer.
Joe is fast on his feet. Joe can kick
the soccer ball and score!

Think It Over

1. What game does Blake like to play?

2. What kind of ball does Joe have?

3. What does Blake show Joe?

4. What does Joe show Cliff?

A New Land for Pop

Vocabulary

Words to Know

I **know what** to **write** on the board.

I **live** in a place called San Francisco.

I am a **citizen** of the United States.

I write my thoughts in my **journal**.

Sight Words

know

what

write

live

Story Words

citizen

journal

Your Turn

Pick one word from either box.

Use the word in a sentence.

Phonics

Wh; Vowel Diphthongs

**Look at each picture.
Read the word.**

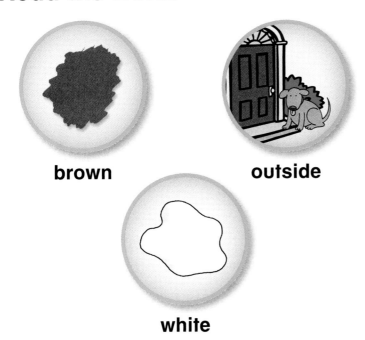

brown

outside

white

Phonics

wh

house

crown

Your Turn

Point to the word that names the picture. Read the word.

own   owl

shout   sheet

moose   mouth

wheel   whale

About the Story

Who is in the story?

Grandfather Pop

Me

Where does the story happen?

old land

new land

A New Land for Pop

by Pam Walker

When my Pop was a boy he liked to read and write. This is his journal.

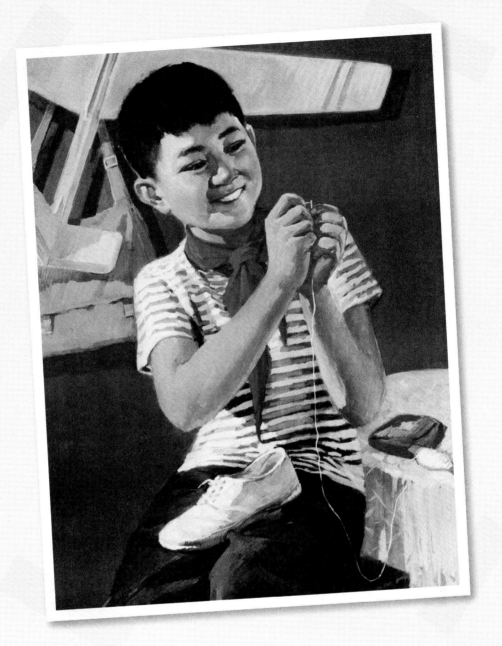

June 1, 1966

Today I got a hole in my white sock. I know what I can do to fix it. Mom will be glad when she sees that I fixed it.

June 4, 1966

Today my mom and I went to a big town. It had a big crowd. I found out a bit about America. I think that I will like our new land.

June 8, 1966

Soon I will see our new home.
Our family will wait at a dock.
They will be glad when Mom and
I land at a dock. They will show
us America.

June 1, 2010

Now I know how to write. I write in my own journal. I tell about fun times with my pop and my dad. I have a lot of fun with my pop and my dad.

June 4, 2010

My pop likes his new land a lot. Pop will soon take a test to become a citizen. Pop still likes to read about his old land and tell me about it. He is my best friend.

June 8, 2010

Today my pop will take a test. Pop will say why he wants to live in this land. If Pop can pass the test, he will be a citizen. Then Pop can vote in his new land. Pop will be so glad, and so will I!

Think It Over

1. Who is Pop?

2. What did Pop like to do as a boy?

3. What did Pop write in his journal?

4. Why will Pop take the test?

A Cowboy's Life

Vocabulary

Words to Know

Could you tell me **where** the school is?

Sight Words

where
worked
again

We **worked** hard at school **again** today.

Story Words

cattle
horse

This cowboy herds **cattle** on his **horse**.

Your Turn

Pick one word from either box.

Use the word in a sentence.

Phonics

Letters: ue, ui, ew

**Look at each picture.
Read the word.**

glue

new

fruit

Your Turn

Name the pictures. Which words have the same sound as the *ue* in **glue**?

223

About the Story

Who is in the story?

cowboys

cowgirl

Where does the story happen?

ranch

A Cowboy's Life

by Duncan McCallister

Let's read about cowboys. A cowboy works on a ranch. Cowboys drive cattle on a few very long trips.

This is a cowboy from the past. His tan hat had a big wide brim. It kept his head dry when rain came down. It kept the sun off his face.

This woman is dressed like a cowboy.
She helped out on a ranch, and she did
a few trick rides. She worked hard, too.

In the past, cowboys were strong. A cowboy needed a strong horse to ride. This cowboy kept a strong grip on a strap to help him steer his horse where he wanted to go.

A cowboy had a strong rope. A cowboy threw the rope on a cow. Then he brought all the cattle to his ranch again. He was glad to be home again. He had a big meal of meat and fruit. The cowboy was tired and glad to take a rest.

Cowboys herded cattle to big ranches. Cowboys had to help cattle cross cold, wet streams. They had to help cattle stay safe.

Cowboys are still strong. We can still see cowboys today. Cowboys still rope and ride just like long ago. Cowboys put on shows. We can go and see trick rides and fun shows. A cowboy is a true hero from the past.

Think It Over

1. What is this story about?

2. Where do cowboys work?

3. What do cowboys do?

4. What did cowboys in the past look like?

Cowboys and Cowgirls

cowboy hat

chaps

rope

boots

▲ This cowboy needs his hat, chaps, and boots on trail rides. He needs a rope to help him, too.

saddle

reins

stirrup

▲ This cowgirl sits on a saddle and puts her feet in stirrups. The reins guide the horse.

Writing

Compare-and-Contrast Writing

Sometimes, authors write to compare two or more things. This kind of writing is called **compare-and-contrast writing**.

Now, cowboys can use trucks in the ranch.

In the past, cowboys didn't have trucks.

Your Turn

Look at the pictures. Which sentence compares both pictures?

1. I don't like to wash the dishes but I do it.

2. You have to use soap to wash dishes.

3. In the past, people didn't have dishwashers, but now they do.

4. A dishwasher is very useful!

Write a Compare-and-Contrast Paragraph

You have read about many kinds of Americans.

Lin wrote about how his kind of fun is different from his grandfather's fun.

> I love playing video games. My grandpa didn't have video games when he was young. He played outdoors with his friends. He loved to play with marbles.

Write!

Work with a partner. Think about your family. What do you do for fun? How is it different from your partner's family?
Write about it.

The Big Question

What do you like most about living in America?

Written

Write about America.

Why is America a good country to live in? What do you do for fun?

Say hello in another language.

People from other countries live in America. Tell some ways people say "hello" in other countries.

Can you act out a story?

Tell a story about your family in America. Use your body and your voice to tell it!

Unit **6**

Friendships

It is nice to have friends! Friends are important in our lives.

Let's Talk

Tell about what
you like to do
with your friends.

What Do You Know about Friendships?

A friend plays with you.

A friend helps you.

A friend cares
for you.

A friend loves you.

Your Turn

Who is your best friend?
Why is your friend special
to you? Tell about it.

243

Sing about Friendships

My Friend, Your Friend

I'm your friend and you are my friend,

each and every day.

I'm your friend and you are my friend.

We sing songs and play fun games.

In our school or in our backyard,

we're as happy as can be.

I'm your friend and you are my friend.

I love you and you love me!

Max and Ray

Vocabulary

Words to Know

Let's all get **together**.

The door is **open**.
Please **come** in!

Sight Words

together

open

come

Susan and I
are **friends**.

We like **music**.

Story Words

friends

music

Your Turn

Pick one word from either box.

Use the word in a sentence.

Phonics

Letters: oo

Look at each picture.
Read the word.

boots

goose

cook

Phonics

moon

book

Your Turn

Point to the word that names the picture.

Read the word.

hook   hack   fat   foot   school   scale   ruff   roof

About the Story

Who is in the story?

Max

Ray

Where does the story happen?

school

Max and Ray

by Scott Carl

illustrated by Anne Kennedy

Meet Max and Ray. Max and Ray are best friends. Max and Ray have a lot of fun in school together.

Max and Ray come together
to fix a big box. The box is open
on top. It has red, blue, and
striped balls. Max and Ray will
tape its side and fix it up.

Max likes math best. He is good
at adding. Max can help Ray count
and add in his math book.

Ray likes spelling best. Ray can spell and print well. He is good at spelling big words. Ray can help Max spell *frog* and *cat* and *jump*.

Max and Ray play cool
music together. Max toots his
sax while Ray claps and sings.

Come on! Tap your foot
and shake your head. Hear the
cool tunes of Max and Ray.

Max and Ray have fun at
school and fun at play. Max
and Ray have fun all day!

Think It Over

1. Who are Max and Ray?

2. What is Max good at?

3. What is Ray good at?

4. What do Max and Ray both like?

Our Park

Vocabulary

Words to Know

Kids share **their** skills with each other.

We **do** something **new every** day!

Welcome to my **neighborhood**! Our **project** is to plant a garden.

Sight Words

their

do

new

every

Story Words

welcome

neighborhood

project

Your Turn

Pick one word from either box.

Use the word in a sentence.

Phonics

R controlled vowels

**Look at each picture.
Read the word.**

car

jar

park

Your Turn

Name the pictures. Which words have the same sound
as the *ar* in **card**?

About the Story

Who is in this story?

neighbors

What is this story about?

This story is about making a new park.

Our Park

by Tyler Beacker
illustrated by Linda Pierce

Welcome! This is our town.
This is a neighborhood in our town.
Our town is a good town, and we
will make it the best town it can be.

Our friends and families meet to plan
a project. We will make a new park.
It will take time. But it will be fun, too.
Kids will enjoy our new park.

We all help make a fine park.
We dig holes and lift beams.

We paint, and we rake. We
do our share to show we care.

Take a look! Our neighborhood has a new park! It is a fun place where families can get together. People can meet their friends.

Everyone can play and eat.
We ride bikes and skate. We eat
hot dogs and corn on the cob.

Our park has a big playground, too. It has fun toys in it. It has a swing, a slide, and a sandbox. We worked hard and we worked together. Every town needs a nice park.

Think It Over

1. What is this story about?

2. What is the project for the neighborhood?

3. What toys are in the playground?

4. Who can enjoy the new park?

Owen and Mzee

Vocabulary

Words to Know

Look **over** the babies carefully.
Each **baby** is **different**.

Sight Words

over

baby

different

A **hippopotamus**
is a big animal.

A **tortoise** carries
its own house!

Story Words

hippopotamus

tortoise

Your Turn

Pick one word from either box.

Use the word in a sentence.

270

Phonics

R controlled vowels

Look at each picture.
Read the word.

curl

burn

winter

Your Turn

Name the pictures. Which words have the same sound you hear in *fern*?

About the Story

Who is in the story?

Mzee

(tortoise)

Owen

(hippopotamus)

What is this story about?

The story is about two friends.

Owen and Mzee

by Morgan Joyce

273

Owen

Mzee

Meet Owen and Mzee.
They are different, but they
are a family.

Owen is a hippopotamus that
has lost his herd. Owen stays close
to Mzee. Mzee is like his dad.

Mzee is green and brown and
has a hard shell. Look at him stick
his neck out of his shell.

Mzee is 120 years old! A
tortoise has a very long life.

Owen is a baby hippopotamus. This hippopotamus is just one year old!

A hippopotamus plays in dirt
and grass. A mom or dad must
help keep him safe.

Owen is still small for a
hippopotamus. Can you see
him in this big grass?

Can you see this little
hippopotamus play in big,
big grass?

Mzee will look over Owen and keep him safe. Owen will not be sad and will not get hurt.

This hippopotamus and this tortoise are a good family. They stay together day and night.

Think It Over

1. Who is Mzee?

2. Who is Owen?

3. Why does Owen need a dad?

4. What will Mzee do for Owen?

Tortoises

Giant tortoise

▲ Tortoises are related to turtles. They live on land. A hard shell protects a tortoise. Tortoises hide in their shells.

284

Mother tortoise

hatchling

▲ This baby tortoise is called a hatchling. It weighed only about 3 pounds at birth. It will stay with its mother until it can take care of itself.

Activity to Do!

Draw a tortoise.

- Label its head.
- Label its feet.
- Label its shell.

Then color your tortoise.

285

Persuasive Writing

You can write to convince someone about something. Imagine you want to convince your parents to allow you to do something.

> I should go to summer camp.
>
> I will learn about nature there.
>
> At summer camp, I will not watch TV all day!

Your Turn

Read each sentence.

Which sentence convinces someone of something?

1. I want to go to camp.

2. In camp I will learn many things.

3. My best friend is going to camp.

Write a Persuasive Paragraph

Pam wrote this persuasive paragraph.

What does she want?

> You have to come to
> my party! There will
> be games. I will have
> prizes for everybody.
> You will have fun.

Write!

Think about something you want to convince your friends about. What is it? Why is it important to you? Write about it.

The Big Question

What makes a good friend?

Written

Write about a friend.

Who is your friend? When did you meet your friend? What do you do together? Write about it.

**Talk about
your friends.**

**Act out what you
do with your friends.**

Tell the class about
your friends and what
makes them special.

Act out a favorite
game or activity you
like to do with friends.

A
B
C
D
E
F
G
H
I
J
K
L
M
N
O
P
Q
R
S
T
U
V
W
X
Y
Z

about ▶ ball

 A

about

Tim asks a question **about** math.

after

He took the pumpkin home **after** he picked it.

again

I visit my family **again**.

all

We **all** worked in the garden.

America

We live in **America**.

another

Here comes **another** friend.

B

baby

This is a **baby**.

backpack

I wear my **backpack** to school.

ball

I play with my **ball**.

be

Getting mail can **be** fun.

because

Ducks swim **because** they live in water.

before

Nan hugged Tip **before** he left.

birds

Birds eat seeds on the ground.

blossom

It is a pretty **blossom**.

blue

The water is **blue**.

bought

He **bought** a snack.

butterfly

A **butterfly** has big wings.

A
B
C
D
E
F
G
H
I
J
K
L
M
N
O
P
Q
R
S
T
U
V
W
X
Y
Z

A
B
C
D
E
F
G
H
I
J
K
L
M
N
O
P
Q
R
S
T
U
V
W
X
Y
Z

C

carnival

We go to the **carnival**.

cattle

The **cattle** are in a field.

celebration

A **celebration** is a special time.

citizen

He is a **citizen** of the United States of America.

come

He will **come** to take Jimmy's letter.

costume

We wear a **costume**.

D

delicious

Chicken is a **delicious** food.

different

Owen and Mzee are **different** animals.

do

Meg and Sam each **do** a different job.

doctor

The **doctor** helps me get well.

duckling

The **duckling** is small.

E

every

My class says the Pledge of Allegiance **every** morning.

F

feathers

Birds have **feathers**.

first

Dad cut the turkey **first**.

food chain

Plants and animals are part of the **food chain**.

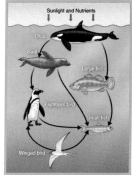

friend

He is my **friend**.

frog

A **frog** jumps and swims.

A
B
C
D
E
F
G
H
I
J
K
L
M
N
O
P
Q
R
S
T
U
V
W
X
Y
Z

293

from

Joe takes a soccer ball **from** his bag.

fun

A party is **fun**.

green

This balloon is **green**.

grow

We water the plants so they will **grow**.

have

They **have** a ball.

he

He helps Tracey cross the street.

hippopotamus

A **hippopotamus** is a big animal.

horses

Horses pull the cart.

A B C D E F G H I J K L M N O P Q R S T U V W X Y Z

I

is

Ted **is** fat.

like

I **like** bedtime.

little

The dog is **little**.

J

journal

I write in a **journal**.

live

I **live** in a busy city.

K

know

I **know** how to sew.

living

The tree is **living**.

L

letter

Jim writes a **letter** to send to José.

look

I **look** far away.

A
B
C
D
E
F
G
H
I
J
K
L
M
N
O
P
Q
R
S
T
U
V
W
X
Y
Z

M

mail

I got a letter in the **mail**.

many

There are **many** bees in the tree.

me

Kelly gave a snack to **me**.

moon

The **moon** is out at night.

music

A horn can make **music**.

my

I wear **my** new backpack to school.

N

neighborhood

I live in a **neighborhood**.

new

That hat is **new**.

O

of

I have a lot **of** friends.

one

Joe has **one** soccer ball.

open

The baby's mouth is **open**.

our

Our flag is on the moon.

out

Dave holds his hands **out**.

over

Can she go **over** the bar?

P

parade

They played in a **parade**.

people

The **people** can smile.

project

We worked on a **project**.

297

A
B
C
D
E
F
G
H
I
J
K
L
M
N
O
P
Q
R
S
T
U
V
W
X
Y
Z

pumpkin

The **pumpkin** is round.

---

ranches

Cattle live on **ranches**.

---

school

I like to go to **school**.

see

I **see** Ted. Ted sees me.

she

She is a vet.

sleigh

The **sleigh** is on snow!

snack

This **snack** tastes good.

so

The turkey is **so** big.

soccer

I play **soccer**.

298

Thanksgiving

Thanksgiving is an American holiday.

the

The girl likes her drink.

their

Eagles use **their** wings to fly.

then

I do my work. **Then** I go out to play.

they

They sort mail.

this

This letter is for Billy.

three

I eat **three** times a day.

3

to

Stan likes **to** drum.

together

Max and Ray solve the problem **together**.

A B C D E F G H I J K L M N O P Q R S **T** U V W X Y Z

too

The hat is **too** big.

tortoise

A **tortoise** is slow.

two

There are **two** boys and **two** balls.

 U

use

Use a helmet to be safe!

V

very

The bird is **very** quick.

 W

waddle

A duck can **waddle**.

wants

The duckling **wants** to come out of the egg.

water

Water is in a lake.

welcome

Welcome to our home!

what

What does the boy like to do?

where

Where do you live? Do you live in the United States?

white

The egg is **white**.

why

Why are the plants near the window?

with

We ate **with** each other.

worked

We **worked** hard in school.

write

Sally likes to **write** in her journal.

 Y

you

I show the book to **you**.

A B C D E F G H I J K L M N O P Q R S T U V W X Y Z

Credits

ILLUSTRATORS: Kathryn Mitter 10–19 Don Tate 22–31 Kathy Wilburn 32–33 Mary Roja 36–43 Daniel Delvalle 45, 89 Bob Masheris 52–53 Apryl Stott 56–57, 59– 65 Sue Miller 58, 78–85 Barbara Spurll 68–75 Olga and Aleksey Ivanov 96–97 Joe LeMonnier 112 Lyuba Bogan 146–147 Linda Holt Ariss 162, 172–173 Drew-Brook Cormack176–185 Marilyn Janovitz 194–195 Mark Stephens 198–209 Melanie Siegel 244–245 Anne Kennedy 248–257 Linda Pierce 260–269.

COVER: Bryan Ballinger

ICONS: Bill Melvin

LETTER LOGOS: Jan Bryan-Hunt

UNIT 1: 2–3 Blend Images/PunchStock; 4 top, Ellen Senisi; 4 top inset, PhotoEdit Inc.; 4 bottom left Pearson Learning Photo Studio; 4 bottom right, Creative Eye/MIRA; 5 top, Photo Researchers; 5 top inset Bettman/Corbis; 5 bottom, PhotoEdit Inc.; 6 left, PhotoEdit Inc.; 6 right, Omni-Photo Communications; 7 top, Omni-Photo Communications; 7 bottom, Photodisc/Getty Images; 8 top, PhotoEdit Inc.; 8 bottom, Pearson Learning Photo Studio; 20 top, PhotoEdit Inc.; 20 middle, Dorling Kindersley; 20 bottom, Dorling Kindersley; 34 top, Stockbyte/Getty Images; 34 middle, Stock Connection; 34 bottom, Dorling Kindersley; 44 top, Ellen Senisi; 44 bottom, Camille Tokerud/ The Image Bank/Getty Images; 46 Owen Franken/Corbis.

UNIT 2: 48–49 Kim Karpeles/Alamy; 50 top, PhotoEdit Inc.; 50 bottom, Photo Researchers; 51 top, Aurora & Quanta Productions; 51 middle, Ellen Senisi; 51 bottom, Dorling Kindersley; 54 top, Photodisc/Getty Images; 54 bottom, PhotoEdit Inc.; 66 top, Creative Eye/MIRA; 66 bottom, Image Bank/Getty Images; 76 top, Dorling Kindersley; 76 bottom, PhotoTake NYC; 86 top, PhotoEdit Inc.; 86 middle, PhotoEdit Inc.; 86 bottom, Liason/Getty Images; 87 top, Robert Harbison; 87 bottom , Photodisc/ Getty Images; 88 top Creative Eye/MIRA; 88 bottom, David R. Frazier Photolibrary; 90–91 Dorling Kindersley; 91 inset, Photodisc/Getty Images.

UNIT 3: 92–93 SuperStock; 94 top, AP Wide World; 94 bottom, PhotoEdit Inc.; 95 top, William Hart/Stone/Getty Images; 95 bottom, Paul Barton; 98 top, PhotoEdit Inc.; 98 middle, Dorling Kindersley; 98 bottom, PhotoEdit Inc.; 100 Brand X Pictures; 102 Altrendo Images/Getty Images; 103 Brand X Images; 104 Donald Nausbaum/Getty Images; 105 bkgd, Sven Creutzman/Corbis; 105 inset, Mike King/Corbis; 106 Photo Researchers; 107 NASA; 108 Getty Images; 109 NASA; 110 top, Stockbyte/Getty Images; 110 bottom, Steve Bly/The Image Bank/Getty Images; 112 top left, John Henley/Corbis; 112 top right, Jason Lee/ Reuters/Corbis; 112 bottom left, Owen Franken/Corbis; 112 bottom right, Fritz CurzonArena/Topham/The Image Works Inc.; 113 bkgd, Jason Lee/ Reuters/Corbis; 113 foreground, Krzysztof Dydynski/Lonely Planet Images; 114, Tony Freeman/PhotoEdit Inc.; 115 bkgd, Jason Lee/Reuters/Corbis; 115 foreground, Krzysztof Dydynski/Lonely Planet Images; 116–117 L. Dantas/Abril/Zefa/Corbis; 116 inset, Owen Franken/Corbis; 117 inset, Jeff Greenberg/The Image Works Inc.; 118–119, Joe Drivas/Getty Images; 118 inset, John Henley/Corbis; 120 Fritz CurzonArena/Topham/The Image Works Inc.; 121 Owen Franken/Corbis; 122 top, National Geographic; 122 bottom, Liason/Getty Images; 123 top, Stock Connection; 123 bottom, Viesti Associates; 124 top, Tom & Dee Ann McCarthy/Corbis; 124 middle PhotoEdit Inc.; 124 bottom, Omni-Photo Communications; 126 top left, Bettmann/Corbis; 126 top middle left, PhotoEdit Inc.; 126 top middle right, Stock Connection; 126 top right, Davis-Lynn Images/Corbis; 126 bottom left, PhotoEdit Inc.; 126 bottom right, Corbis NY 127 Stone Allstock/Getty Images; 128 PhotoEdit Inc.; 129 Bettmann/Corbis; 130 PhotoEdit Inc.; 131 Corbis NY; 132 Stock Connection; 133 PhotoEdit Inc.; 134–135 Davis-Lynn Images/Corbis; 136 Stone Allstock/Getty Images; 137 PhotoEdit Inc.; 138 Stockbyte/Getty Images; 140–141 PhotoEdit Inc.; 140 Bettmann/Corbis.

UNIT 4: 142–143 Nora Good/Masterfile; 144 top, Stock Connection; 144 bottom, Photodisc/Getty Images; 145 top, Dorling Kindersley; 145 middle, Agence France Presse/Getty Images; 145 bottom, Dorling Kindersley; 148 top, PhotoEdit Inc.; 148 middle, Bettmann/Corbis;148 bottom, Photo Researchers; 150 top left, Steve Shott/DK Images; 150 top right, Barrie Watts/DK Images; 150 bottom, Mary Rhodes/Animals Animals/Earth Scenes; 151–153 Barrie Watts/DK Images; 154 Jane Burton/DK Images; 155 Steve Shott/DK Images; 156 Barrie Watts/DK Images; 157 Mary Rhodes/Animals Animals/Earth Scenes; 158–159 Barrie Watts/DK Images; 160 top, Dorling Kindersley; 160 middle, Dorling Kindersley; 160 bottom, Ambient Images; 162 top left, Cathy Melloan, Brian Mullenix/Alamy Images; 162 top right, Royalty Free/Corbis; 162 middle left, Royalty Free/Corbis; 162 middle, DK Images; 162 middle right, Ian O'Leary/DK Images; 163 Cathy Melloan, Brian Mullenix/Alamy Images; 164 Cathy Melloan; 165 top, Brian Mullenix/Alamy Images; 165 bottom, DK Images; 166 Cathy Melloan; 167 Royalty Free/Corbis; 168 Photolibray Pty. Ltd./Index Open; 169 Photodisc/Getty Images; 170 Ian O'Leary/DK Images; 171 Cathy Melloan; 174 all, Dorling Kindersley; 186 top left, Photo Researchers; 186 top middle, Photo Researchers; 186 top right, Photo Researchers; 186 bottom, Dorling Kindersley; 188–189, Dorling Kindersley; 188 inset, EMG Education Management Group.

UNIT 5: 190–191 Billy Hustace/Stone/Getty Images; 192 top, Dorling Kindersley; 192 bottom, Dorling Kindersley; 193 top, Ted Spiegel/CORBIS; 193 middle Dorling Kindersley; 193 bottom, Dorling Kindersley; 196 top, PhotoEdit Inc.; 196 middle, Peter Arnold; 196 bottom, Mark Seelan/zefa/ Corbis; 210 top, David Roth/Stone/Getty Images; 210 top middle, Dorling Kindersley; 210 bottom middle, PhotoEdit Inc.; 210 bottom, PhotoEdit Inc.; 212 top left, Randy Faris/Corbis; 212 top right, Randy Faris/Corbis; 212 bottom left, Franklin McMahon/Corbis; 212 bottom right, Swim Ink/Corbis; 213 Randy Faris/Corbis; 214 Bettmann/Corbis; 215 Swim Ink/Corbis; 216 Franklin McMahon/Corbis; 217 Swim Ink/Corbis; 218–220 Randy Faris/Corbis; 221 Swim Ink/Corbis; 222 top, Taxi/Getty Images; 222 middle, PhotoEdit Inc.; 222 bottom, Viesti Associates; 224 top left, Royalty-Free/Corbis; 224 top right Bill Manns/The Art Archive; 224 bottom, Bettmann/Corbis; 225 Royalty-Free/Corbis; 226 Bettmann/Corbis; 227 Bettmann/Corbis; 228 Bill Manns/The Art Archive; 229 Library of Congress; 230 The Granger Collection, NY; 231 Bettmann/Corbis; 232 Bill Manns/Corbis; 233 Bettmann/Corbis; 234 Doring Kindersley; 235, Dorling Kindersley; 236 top, National Geographic; 236 middle, Pearson Education; 236 bottom, Bettmann/Corbis; 238 Ellis Ashkenazi.

UNIT 6: 240–241 Bill Bachmann/PhotoEdit Inc. Inc.; 242 top, PhotoEdit Inc.; 242 bottom, Elizabeth Crews Photography; 243 top, PhotoEdit Inc.; 243 bottom, Photolibrary; 246 top, Silver Burdett Ginn; 246 middle, Photodisc/Getty Images; 246 bottom, Jutta Klee/Corbis; 258 top, Photo Researchers; 258 bottom, PhotoEdit Inc.; 270 top Photodisc/Getty Images; 270 middle Dorling Kindersley; 270 bottom, Dorling Kindersley; 272 left, National Geographic; 272 right, National Geographic; 273 Peter Greste/Reuters/Corbis; 274 left, National Geographic; 274 right, Omni-Photo Communications; 275 AP Wide World Photos; 276 Dorling Kindersley; 277 National Geographic; 278-279 Dorling Kindersley; 280–281 National Geographic; 282 Peter Greste/Reuters/Corbis; 283 Peter Greste/Reuters/Corbis; 284 Omni-Photo Communications; 285 Animals Animals/Earth Scenes; 286 Ellen Senisi; 287–288 Merrill Education; 287 inset, Dorling Kindersley.